I LOVE you MORE

To Jill, for your endless
love and support.

C.H.W.

To baby Lucia.

K. & K.H.

I LOVE YOU MORE

Clare Helen Welsh

Kevin & Kristen Howdeshell

nosy crow

"Goodnight, sleep tight, my precious one,"
said Mum to little Rae.

"And know I love you more
than I can find the words to say . . .

I love you like the penguins love
to waddle in the snow,

like seal pups love to snooze
upon their sunlit icy floe.

I love you like the mighty eagle
loves to soar and glide,

like goats and foxes love to climb
the sky-high mountainside.

I love you like the turtles love
to surf and sweep and roam,

like fish of every colour love
their underwater home.

I love you like the lizard loves
the rocky, sun-warmed land,

like humpbacked camels love
the desert's softly shifting sand.

I love you like the wolf cubs love
to laze and play in caves,

like moose love swimming swiftly
through the rushing river waves.

I love you like the tiny tree frogs
love to leap up high,

like winged things love to flutter
and like parrots love to fly.

I love you like the dolphins love
the peaceful, boundless sea . . .

. . . like lions love to race and roar,
like leopards love their tree.

Like pandas love to
peep and climb . . .

. . . like blue whales
love to blow . . .

. . . I think I love you more than
it is possible to show.

Unless . . ." said Mum.

"Let's count the stars,
count each and every light.

Then count the sparkly planets shining
brightly in the night.

That's how much I love you,
more than all the many stars,
more than all the planets,
more than Jupiter or Mars."

“That IS a lot,” said little Rae.
“You love me more than space,
more than any sun or moon
or any thing or place,

as much as any creature loves
the sea, the land or shore . . .

but there's one thing
that you should know . . .

. . . I think
I love you more."

First published 2024 by Nosy Crow Ltd
Wheat Wharf, 27a Shad Thames,
London, SE1 2XZ, UK

Nosy Crow Eireann Ltd
44 Orchard Grove, Kenmare,
Co Kerry, V93 FY22, Ireland

www.nosycrow.com

ISBN 978 1 83994 417 8 (HB)
ISBN 978 1 83994 419 2 (PB)

A CIP catalogue record for this book is available from the British Library.

Printed in China.
Papers used by Nosy Crow are made from wood grown in sustainable forests.

1 3 5 7 9 8 6 4 2 (HB)
1 3 5 7 9 8 6 4 2 (PB)